I AM PSYCHIC, NOT TELEPATHIC

A Psychic's Story Book III

AURIEL GRACE

Edited by
ADRIENNE HORN

A Gang of Girls Inc.

CONTENTS

I am Psychic, Not Telepathic   v

1. I am Psychic Not Telepathic   1
2. Psychic Kids   7
   The Egg   11
   Monster Spray   13
   The Clair's   15
3. Inner Guidance   19
   Assignment   23
   Notes   25
4. Being Present   27
   Be Truthful   29
   Assignment   31
   Notes   33
5. Assignment   35
   Notes   39
6. Mirror Work   41
   Notes   45
7. Spirit Guides and Angels   47
   Fairy Godmother   51
   Notes   55
   Guardian Angel   57
   Notes   61
8. What is an Energy Vampire   63
9. Boundaries and Self Preservation   67
10. Home is Sanctuary   71
   Notes   75
11. Intention and Living Intentionally   77
   Assignment   83
   Notes   85
12. Crystals & Pendulums   87
   Using a Pendulum   89

Notes   91

Crystals, Gems & Minerals   93

13. Playing and Simplifying   97

Notes   101

14. Equal Exchange of Energy   103

15. Are You Present?   107

Glossary of Terms   109

About the Author   115

Other books by Auriel Grace –   117

I AM PSYCHIC, NOT TELEPATHIC

A Psychic's Story Book III

I dedicate this book to my 'Ohana – my Family –

Vicki 'Star' Harding, Mom, Jessica Ia, Sandy Kusy (AKA TigerLady), My Bro THEO, Cindy 'LiteHope' Moss, Rockin Reverend Rhonda and Mike Schienle, Bambi Harris, Molly Jones, Katie Girl, Ella Bo Bella, Gunnar, Anissa and Mark Chmura, Melinda Carver, Kris & Pauli Sedersten, Kat Hobson, Hanna – Sunshine Girl – O'Dell, Darla Tegtmeier, Susan and Tracy 'Batman' Todd, Lisa V. So many more!

Special Thanks to Adrienne Horne for her patience!

I AM PSYCHIC NOT TELEPATHIC

My great grandfather died when I was five years old. I remember waking up, seeing him standing at the end of my bed. He smiled and waved at me. Then walked out of my bedroom. I got out of bed and found my mother and great grandmother crying along with other members of my family, in the living room of our house.

My mother told me my grandpa died, we would not see him again. She explained to me he was in heaven and he wouldn't come back. I looked at my Gran and she agreed. I was five years old and trusted what my elders told me.

I saw and spoke to other spirits during my childhood who looked very physical and were mysteriously unseen to my Grandmother, mother and others. These spirits usually had good advice and were fun to play with.

I was raised as a Roman Catholic. The masses my family attended were very enjoyable. We were lucky to have good priests and nuns at all of the churches we attended. I became a Catechism teacher at sixteen years old. I taught the first grade and it was very fun for me and the class.

During this time, I spoke to the Mother Superior about

becoming a nun. I thought if I could live the life a nun I could find answers I needed to understand who I was 'seeing', 'hearing', and 'feeling'. The Mother Superiors advice to me was – Ask for guidance and trust it will be given. – she reminded me of my great connection to the Creator.

My spiritual education started in my twenties. My cousin started to channel an extra-terrestrial named Ah-Tu. Ah –Tu inspired my education in trusting, using my instincts and intuition. Ah-Tu spoke of the Universe as our neighborhood and to start seeing ourselves as multi-dimensional beings. The first time my cousin channeled Ah-Tu, I asked about my Grandmother who was having health problems. He told me not to worry and reminded me the soul of every living being is eternal. Something clicked in my brain and I understood. I understood if my grandmother passed through the veils she didn't ceased to exist. She changed form, that's it! We are infinite – Isn't that wonderful?

I started reading everything I could about alternative lifestyles, spirit guides, angels and fairies, meditation, prayer, being present, mediumship and channeling. I wanted answers for and about myself, my surroundings and all living entities seen and unseen.

After studying on my own for about ten years I intended a teacher to come forth so I could focus on expanding and deepening my understanding of how to use my intuition and instinct for the highest and greatest good of myself and my family.

A teacher came to me when I was ready to really devote myself to my chosen path. At the time, I chose to be the best intuitive I could be.

She, my teacher gave me a great foundation and so much more.

After her, there were more teachers. I continued my education. What I learned is written in these pages.

What will you find while you read these pages?

You will find information about intuition, spirit guides, angels, crystals, energy, intention and what do to with these tools. If you are a parent, aunt, uncle, grandparent, friend or relative of a psychic kid there is some good information in these pages about them as well.

I always tell people your intuition is like a muscle, you have to exercise to keep it in shape. I always give homework to my clients. It is entirely up to you to do the homework written in these pages.

I am Psychic, Not Telepathic

A couple of weeks ago I was sitting in a lawyer's office asking for advice. She asked me what I did professionally, I told her I am a psychic.

She was surprised and said well you probably have known all along what I am thinking!

I said, no, I am psychic, not telepathic. I can't tell what you are thinking. I am not really interested in your thoughts. I am interested in your advice as to how to proceed with the issue at hand.

I think it is pretty funny how people still are not aware of what psychics are and how we receive information.

I love what I do. I help many people, the best thing I do is help to resolve issues and give Hope. Hope is a powerful gift to people who are wanting to remove or resolve whatever is going on in their lives. It is beautiful to watch as people have their realizations about themselves. After the realization, they shift and move into the energy of transition and Hope.

So, psychic's, at least this psychic doesn't read minds. I receive information in what I call a 'download'. Then I interpret the 'download' as best as I can to the client. Sometimes it is what they want to hear, most of the times it is information their guides and angels want to give them or be aware of.

It's ok if you look at me and it is ok if you talk to me. What goes on in your mind is none of my business. I don't look for your secrets, not my business.

My business is to give you messages for your higher and better good and answer your questions with the best of my abilities as a translator for the etheric realm.

With that being said, I am really good at tuning into your energy. I can tell when clients are locked down and looking to be amazed by not saying anything to me. I find that also funny! If you are paying for a reading and you want a good one, open up so you can actually hear the interpretation of what your spirit guides and angels have to say to you.

Ask questions, so you can get the answers you so want and desire.

Psychics are not omniscient. We don't know everything, personally I don't want that responsibility.

The Creator is Omniscient.

We are vessels waiting to be filled with information to give to you.

I want to remind you, not everything is written in stone. Every time you have a reading your attitude

changes on the subject as you are receiving information to help you make decisions.

You always have a choice. You have to give yourself permission to make the choice or choices!

I am a psychic, soul retrieval practitioner, author, radio hostess and metaphysical teacher. I help people with their clarity and intuitive skills on many levels. They learn and remember their direct connection to their Divine Source and the connectedness of the whole while working with me.

Many people feel like they have done bad. They do not feel worthy of their connection to their Divine Source.

You are worthy of your direct connection to your Divine Source.

Acknowledge and be that connection.

Everyone is intuitive. How intuitive are you? How intuitive are your children?

Are you interested in exploring your intuitive skills?

Read on, I promise it will be fun for you!

Are you ready for a new adventure?

PSYCHIC KIDS

What or who is a psychic kid? You were probably a psychic kid. Now you have psychic kids.

There are a lot of titles for them. When I 'see' them I don't see titles I see a human with extraordinary abilities.

As a child, I was and still am Clairvoyant and Clairaudient. I see and I hear, predominantly. When I was a little girl, when I did see spirits, they appeared as they did in life. They looked like real people to me. So, until I was about twelve years old, I thought this was a normal event in all people's lives. I was not afraid of them as they recognized I could see them. Sometimes I received messages to give to family members or friends. That I think was the most difficult for me, to give the messages in a roundabout way, so no one knew where the message came from.

My great grandmother Georgia, realized I had intuitive abilities and would ask me if it was my 'special feeling'. She was the only one who accepted my abilities and we kept it between us.

Now when parents come to me and ask me - what do I do and Is this real?

I say, what do you want to do? Yes, it is real.

As a parent, you can support your child and teach them how to be courageous. Explain they have a gift. Be present with them when they speak to you about their intuitive gift. Ask questions and allow the answers. When you are open with your child in this way it is a true gift!

Grandparents, if your children are not open for the experience yet, spend time with your grandchildren and allow the conversations. Remind your grandchild this is your special time together.

Grandparents speak to your children, ask them to be open minded and allow their child to be the wondrous light they are.

Do your research, read, talk to intuitive people for advice on what to do with your intuitive child. There is a lot of information out there. Ask your child what it is they are feeling, seeing or hearing, what do they 'know'? Do your best to follow through. Support is great and also remember there are other interests that need to be addressed too.

Psychic kids need balance, they need structure and understanding, just like most children.

Best advice for a parent is to ask questions, if you ask questions, you will get answers.

Being intuitive is the most natural way to be for every-body. The Creator(s) gave us these abilities to assist us with our lives! You too are intuitive, be present pay attention and allow your gifts to flow.

Most of the 'assignments' in this book you can share with your children. Try the assignments with them, you will be surprised at the results. I know I am a parent of psychic kids too.

Here are some ideas for you and your family to consider as you move about your day. I always recommend these two ideas to start parents of psychic kids. Most kids are open and comfortable with the ideas.

For Empathic Children - Ask them how they feel, then have the child touch your hand and tell you how you feel. If there are more family members in the house have your child touch each person to figure out how they feel. Your child will start to learn how to discern their own feelings from others feelings. That is very important for an empath.

Empathic people tend to 'carry' a lot of energy that is not their own. Recognizing you are empathic and under-standing you don't need to 'carry' other people 'stuff', helps your child with their own clarity. That is a blessing in itself.

THE EGG

The Egg is a way to protect yourself and your family from unwelcome energies. The Egg can be any color or colors you want. I recommend mirrored colors for children and people who work in service type jobs, social services, military, police, firemen etc. We do this so the energies absolutely will not enter your personal space.

My Egg is metallic pastel pink, most of the time. When I feel, I am going to a place that is haunted or has negative energy, I will fluff my egg out about three to five feet around me. This way I am not affected by the energies within the space.

1. Have each family member visualize an egg around the physical body.

2. Let your children know their body-eggs can be any color they want, sparkly or metallic, but they have to be dense. The Density or deep color of the egg shape helps keep negative energy from attaching or getting close to the person.

3. Help them with these images by visualizing what they are describing to you. Reinforce their visualizations with

the Intention the egg protects them for their highest and greatest good.

4. Let the children know they can change the color of their body-eggs any time they want too. The eggs can be many colors as long as they remain dense.

5. You can do this protective work with your house, car, mother, boyfriend, husband, wife, sister-in-law—anyone you know.

What does your egg look like?

What does each of your family member's egg look like?

A beautiful young lady was having problems with unwanted energies. We were able to clear up her energetic field and her problems were resolved. She was taught how to visualize her Egg and since then she has not had any problems. She was one of our best students at the meta-physical school

MONSTER SPRAY

Children have wild imaginations. They are open to possibilities. There are a lot of children and adults who are afraid of the dark. Monster spray can help keep the 'monsters' away.

One of the ingredients in Monster Spray is Roses. The scent of roses is the highest vibrational smell on the planet. That's why we give roses to our love ones. Roses represent our love and the smell is associated with love. Love is the highest vibration and it can heal all ailments. To combat monsters, you use the smell of love, roses.

The next ingredient is salt. Salt absorbs residual energy, negativity, anger, frustration and sorrow. Salt is a great energy balancer.

Spring or rain water, use good water for this spray. Water is a great cleanser. You can pray with the water asking Mother Mary to bless the water.

Lavender to help us relax.

When your child doesn't want to go to bed for fear, spray the room. Put a smaller spray bottle in the room for them to use when they are afraid.

Teaching yourself and your children to say to bothersome spirits.

I am a child of God – Be gone!

This assists the child with claiming their space, and gives them confidence they are protected.

THE CLAIR'S

I am starting with the Clair's, that's what I call them. The Clair's describe our intuitive gifts very clearly hence the word Clair. I am mostly clairaudient, I prefer to hear or know, claircognizant, seeing can be distracting for me while I am doing intuitive work. Yes, you can have more than one gift and you can choose how you want to receive information.

When I clear haunted houses or property I can smell the spirits before I get there. What do they smell like? Musty, that is a great way to describe them. I smell them out and get them to where they need to go. I am a 'travel agent' for spirits.

I am not a traditional psychic medium. I do not assist with closure for your friends and family who have crossed over. I do hear from the spirit world quite a bit, but not like that. It is a choice I made, you can make that choice as well as your children.

Everyone on this planet has 'free will' you always have a choice. It is very important you remember you have free will. There are a great many intuitive people who want to control their clients. Be always aware and if you feel as though an intuitive person is trying to talk you into something you are not comfortable with do not be swayed. Walk away.

Clairalience – Using your nose and your sense of smell, you can retrieve information. Some spirits or properties have a certain scent associated with them. Clairalience is the ability to detect these scents.

Clairaudience – To hear intuitively past our three-dimensional world clearly, hearing those who have passed over, Angels, guides, etc.

Clair cognizance – 'Clear Knowing' is the ability to recognize and receive information from the ethers, intuitively you 'know' the information is correct. Most Prophets are Claircognizant.

Clairgustance – 'You can literally taste it.' Clairgustance is the ability to taste information.

Clairsentience – 'Psychometry' is the ability to feel or touch objects or persons and receive knowledge about those objects or a person's story.

Clairvoyance – The ability to see past our three-dimensional world clearly. For example: Ghosts, Angels, Fairies, Spirit Guides, etc.

Now that you know the different Clair's, you might feel more comfortable with your own gifts. Be practical with the information you receive and give out. Always be discerning when dealing with your gifts or others gifts.

We will be talking about the Clair's as we move through this book. Consider each one and reach back into your memories to see which ones you have utilized the most without realizing the gift.

Many times, we disregard what we see, feel, hear or know. We tend to move along our days in a habitual manner.

Try this, when you get the message you need to go somewhere or make a right turn instead of a left, consider following through with the message. Your inner guidance or spirit guides are going to always steer you in the correct direction, that's their job allow them to assist you.

If I didn't listen to my inner guidance and learn to have confidence in what I was feeling, hearing and knowing, I would not have had the adventurous life I have lived and am still living.

INNER GUIDANCE

What is inner guidance or your inner compass?

It is the feeling in the pit of your stomach letting you know there is something you need to pay attention too. It is the dream you remember vividly giving you direction(s) for your life. It is the feeling of Déjà vu or recurring thoughts.

The question is – do you listen to your inner guidance or do you dismiss it?

When you start following your inner guidance, you will find your life starts to flow easier and you are in a clearer state of mind. Trust what you are hearing, feeling or seeing. You are the only one who can act on your intuition or inner guidance. It is a practice and a lesson in trusting the self.

It doesn't matter your age, sex, religion, color etc., You have the ability to listen to yourself and follow through with your brilliant ideas. Your friends and family who love and accept you, will support you in all your endeavors.

I write these ideas in present terms because it is happening now. More and more people are seeking their truths and seeing the connectedness in all living beings,

overcoming their fears of the unknown and loving themselves unconditionally.

That is how the real journey begins in loving the self.
Love can transform everything in your life, so love yourself
and follow through with your inner guidance and instinct.

How do you listen to your inner guidance? Or intuition? You practice connecting to your higher self and
Divine Source. You practice being present and loving yourself enough to practice. In this way, you can be the greatest
example for your children, your friends and family.

Your experience is what brings you to this moment right
now, in this place where you are, and in this position where
you are now seated. Everything has been in preparation for
this moment.

It is important to pay attention and to BE PRESENT.
You will see this come up from time to time and it is a
reminder to focus.

Here are some inner guidance examples –

When I was thinking about moving from Angel Fire,
New Mexico, a friend of mine handed me a hot springs
book and advised me to check it out. I did, I saw Pagosa
Springs, Colorado in the book. I drove through there the
previous year and remembered how awesome the energy
was. I knew and felt this was the next place I would live.

My youngest son is a wild child and always in trouble.
One day I really felt like he should not leave our apartment
complex, very strongly. I told him so and he said he would
not. I went to run errands and when I got back my son was
not home. He left a note saying he went to the pool. I
continued my day. When my son did not show for dinner or
answer his phone, I got worried and called his girlfriend
who also had not heard from him.

Late that night I received a phone call from the

Naperville Police Department. They had arrested my son during a traffic stop, while he was in the car with his friend.

Yesterday, I told Todd to take the car to work today, I had the feeling his tire was not going to make it. His scooter tire was leaking air. I ran a couple of errands before he needed to be at work. He decided to leave five minutes before I arrived home. He needs a new tire now.

There are three examples of intuitive feeling, listening and knowing.

There are those of you wonder why or how people get ahead in their lives, it's because they are attuned and listening to their inner guidance, whether they are aware or not and that how they are able to follow through with their brilliant ideas. Follow through and trust yourself. Now you are aware, practice following through.

You really don't have to do anything fancy to remember your connection to your instinct and intuition, except practice and follow through.

We were meant to come to this planet to have experiences, to live our lives for our own higher and better good.

ASSIGNMENT

I love my phone, my phone helps me connect to my friends, family and clients through many ways. While I am waiting for my coffee, I visualize my phone and dial up. I call upon my spiritual crew to assist me during the day.

A fun way to remind yourself of your connection to your Divine Source, spirit guides and angels is to visualize a phone, dial up and connect to your higher self, spirit guides, angels, Divine Source. This is the energy that assists you to feel full of joy. Do this every day before getting out of bed or when you start to feel afraid or alone.

Find a way to connect with Divine Source, Spirit Guides or Angels so you get guidance straight from Source. Everyone has 'their way'. I like calling people, so it made sense to me to dial up and to stay connected for my highest and best good.

Assignment

Note in your life how you came to connect to your Divine Source, Spirit Guides and Angels.

NOTES

BEING PRESENT

Be present with me!

I deserve your full attention and you deserve mine. Focus and stay in your body while you read this book and throughout your days. This is how you are going to absorb and be able to utilize what you are reading and learning. Here is a simple exercise you can do in order to get in your body.

Take a deep breath. Breathe in your favorite color and start to fill yourself with the color. Start with your toes. Keep filling your physical body with the color until you are full. When you can see, the color coming out of the ends of your hair and the pores of your skin, you're present and in your body.

Think about how you feel. Are you warmer? Are you happier? Are you calmer? Do you feel better? It always feels good to be fully present.

Practice this meditation every day and any time you are not feeling present. This meditation will help you feel grounded and connected. Teach this technique to your children. Ask them how they feel when they are through. Listen to what they say, write it down.

When you are present in your life you are able to steer your way through your day. You make better decisions and you feel more stable. When you are present there is less anxiety, stress, frustration. You are able to strategize and make clear decisions for yourself and family.

If you are a person who finds it easier to be in daydream-land instead of being present during your daily activities, the question to ask yourself is:

"Why don't I like being in this beautiful body on this beautiful earth?"

Start the discovery process by writing down how you feel about yourself and your life;

BE TRUTHFUL

Make two columns, one for the ideas you like about your life and the other column all the ideas you dislike about in your life. This may take some time, so be patient with yourself, keep adding and or subtracting from your lists. Children from twelve and up can also do this exercise.

As you review your lists on the dislike column, ask yourself: How can I release this idea that is no longer serving me. How can I create a better me? It could be as easy as finding a new job, place to live, new friends or new lover, or even just being present with your loved ones.

It isn't an easy task to break old habits that don't serve you. When I have to break a habit or release energy no longer serving me, when I feel that energy come up I say –

I Release you!

For example –
Your friend or family member hurts your feelings

An embarrassing moment

Heartbreak, Heartache

Anger

Frustration

Melancholy

You want to push that energy out of your energy field. You can also have Reiki Treatments, I recommend thirty minutes a month. You also can do a cord cutting ceremony. I recommend cord cutting every six months. This is called maintenance. You are maintaining clarity for yourself.

As you release old ways of being you make room to reinvent yourself. It takes courage to make change in your life. Being present with yourself and your loved ones is the first step as you honor yourself and others by doing so. You will find as you let go you will start feeling lighter and more energetic, willing to try new ideas and ways of being.

Always give yourself permission to expand and grow, listen to your intuition and follow through as you write your list.

Think about each item on your list and as you are more present with the item, you will see resolutions come into your life. Ask for assistance if you need it!

When you update your lists, take the old list and burn it. This is a good way of releasing old thought patterns. You can watch old thought patterns be consumed by the flames of your fire and as you watch say to yourself:

"I release these thought patterns no longer serving me!"

During this process, remember to be grateful for this healing or release.

Remember this is the only lifetime you will be this person, you want to make it an awesome lifetime doing what you want to do and being you! Make it a great lifetime!

ASSIGNMENT

Gratitude expands you, it enhances your life and assists with creating new ways of being. Be grateful for having the courage to be alive on Earth. When you are grateful and present in your life it is easy to be open to your intuition and inner guidance. Your life expands and grows.

I put sticky notes up in strategic places in my home. I see the gratitude's and it makes me feel good. When I feel good, I am able to live with ease and grace.

Write all the things in your life you are grateful for. Put this list where you can see it when you wake up in the morning. Lists can be placed on sticky notes all around the house.

Remember to add to your list when a new gratitude comes up.

Start your list with: I am so very grateful for…

It is a good to realize what you are grateful for. This feeling raises your resonance and helps you feel comfortable and happy. You deserve to be happy and comfortable in your life.

Ask your children to write down what they are grateful for. Place their lists where they can see them. Allow them to add to their lists. This helps them think about their lives. It uplifts them and brings them into the present moment.

NOTES

ASSIGNMENT

When I do readings, reiki or soul retrieval sessions, I connect with the akashic records, my guides and angels to receive messages for you. This assignment will assist you with connecting to your guides and angels to receive information.

You may see symbols, pictures, hear sounds, know or smell something about the person write it down.

You will be surprised at how much information you will receive.

On the next page, you will see two circles. Pick a partner and pick a circle. Take a breath and clear your mind. Now, open yourself up to information about your partner. The 'download' may feel funny, like you are expanding. Then you may see, hear or know the information. The information may come in different ways. Do not judge it or dismiss it. This information isn't about you, it is about your partner. Write down the information in or around the circle you picked for your partner. Then explain to your partner what information you received.

Be Clear and Present

We will start with an easy clearing exercise.

Take a breath and quiet your mind.

Visualize a vortex or tornado circling your feet.

With each breath you take, the vortex rises over your body spinning faster and faster.

As the vortex spins you allow it to pull out of your field all those thoughts and energies that no longer serve you.

Visualize the vortex move up over your legs, hips, core, neck and head until you hear a pop. Your energetic field is now clear!

YAY!

Take a deep breath. Breathe in your favorite color and start to fill yourself with the color. Start with your toes. Keep filling your physical body with the color until you are full.

When you can see, the color coming out the ends of your hair and the pores of your skin, you're present and in your body.

Ask for information for your partners higher and better good – then start writing it down. You will be surprised at your results.

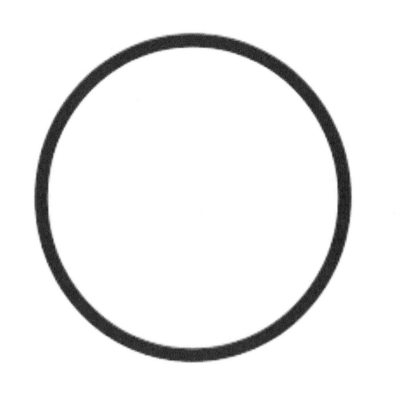

NOTES

MIRROR WORK

Everyone wants to connect to their spirit guides and angels. Everyone has their spiritual crew that assists them. As we grow our crew may change or we become aware of specific guides to assist us with specific projects in our lives. The Archeia Hope assisted me quite a bit through my childhood. She uplifted and encouraged my creativity, my love of reading and writing. As I matured, Archeia Faith, Archeia Grace and Archeia Charity assisted me into adulthood. Archeia Hope is the spokesperson for my guides. After all she is a messenger angel. She has lots of messages, very chatty.

What does Hope look like? She is pink, bubblegum pink to be exact. Pink is a happy color, it is the color of love and friendship. She doesn't take a shape or form usually as she will explain to you in the book Angels – A Psychic's Story, she is energy.

When you are doing this next exercise, you may also be aware of color. Many times, our guides and angels don't take form, they are energy.

Scrying is an ancient way of 'seeing'.

We are going to flex some muscles with this exercise. When you are doing this exercise, you will either be aware or see the energy of your guides and angels.

You know the saying - Magic Mirror on the wall...

Well that's what we are doing except we will be asking to see our guides and angels. When we actually see these wondrous beings of light it helps our connection to them. They become real to us and it is easier to receive messages from them.

This is what you do –

Look into a mirror– say aloud 'I intend to see my spirit guides and angels for my highest and greatest good.' I have a specific mirror I use to scrye with.

Close your eyes, take a breath and quiet your mind.

Ask your guides and angels to gather around you.

Open your eyes, focus on your chin or forehead.

You may see out of the corner of your eyes little flickers. Take a breath and connect with the flickers. You may start to 'see' or 'feel' your guides and angels around you. Do not disregard what you see or feel. Take note of how the energy changes around you as you start to connect. You may feel pressure around your head for a moment.

Try this every day!

The first time I tried it I saw my face get really old. I was relieved as I want to be on the planet for a while. I still have plenty of things to do! If your face changes allow the change. You may see yourself from a past life or what your higher self looks like.

I saw my guardian angel, he is big and blue with metallic wings. I saw the Archeia. Archeia Hope is pink and takes up a lot of space. The more I practiced the more I saw and it was awesome to see their energies around me. You will have this opportunity every time you practice!

Be Clear and Present

We will start with an easy clearing exercise.

Take a breath and quiet your mind.

Visualize a vortex or tornado circling your feet.

With each breath you take, the vortex rises over your body spinning faster and faster.

As the vortex spins, you allow it to pull out of your field all those thoughts and energies that no longer serve you.

Visualize the vortex move up over your legs, hips, core, neck and head until you hear a pop. Your energetic field is now clear!

YAY!

Take a deep breath. Breathe in your favorite color and start to fill yourself with the color. Start with your toes. Keep filling your physical body with the color until you are full.

When you can see the color coming out the ends of your hair and the pores of your skin, you're present and in your body.

Look at yourself in the mirror. Really look at yourself. While you are looking remember you are a multi-dimensional being. There is more to you than your physical presence. Ask to see your guides and Angels, your energy field, chakras.

To do this look at your chin, relax. As you relax you may see flashes of light or movement. Be patient and do this every day. As you get used to you being multi-dimensional, you will start to see more as you are ready.

What do you see? Write it down.

Do this with your children. What do they see? Write it down.

Practice this every day! Recommended 15 minutes.

Do NOT give up!

Let go of the idea of I can't or I am unable. The universe doesn't understand these words, because the universe doesn't understand the negative. When you say "can't", the universe hears "can". When you say "unable" the universe only hears "able".

The reason why the universe acts this way is because the universe doesn't look at words. It looks at resonance. When you resonate ability, it is not a "do or a do not" there is only the is-ness of the ability. You are completely able to do this. It is only by choice do you choose to not do it.

NOTES

SPIRIT GUIDES AND ANGELS

F airy or Elemental – They are the teachers and Guides of the Earth. There are Fairies everywhere. You can also call them elementals.

Sylphs, Air Fairies
Undines, Water Fairies
Salamanders, Fire Fairies
Gnomes, Earth Fairies.

They range in sizes and shapes. What is wondrous about Fairies is there is no hierarchy. All Fairies know their own importance and the importance of all living beings.

The wind blows,
Water flows,
Flowers grow,
Fires Glow

Fairies love children and children love Fairies. When a child says, they are or have been playing with Fairies, believe them. Read up on Fairies, find out about all the different kinds there are and how you can help them. They can help you!

Again, pay attention and be present with your child. Have your child draw or describe the Fairies they are playing with. What are the Fairies telling them? Do your children have interests in insects, flowers, ponds, trees, birds anything to do with nature? Encourage these pursuits, most likely you or your child is being inspired by the Fairies. Some of our greatest scientists, biologists, entomologists, geologists are inspired by Fairies.

This will give you insight to your child and allow you to participate in some fun.

You also might be missing scissors, jewelry, sparkly items, little bits and pieces of games. Let the Fairies know you want these little things back if you need them. You will find them within a couple of days if they borrowed these items.

If you have children, you need to let the Fairies know that a human child needs to sleep. Make a schedule for the Fairies to play with your children so they can sleep. Fairies don't sleep, they are pure energy.

My youngest son was having a hard time falling asleep and staying asleep until he told me the pixies were keeping him awake, they wanted to play with him. We made a sign with construction paper saying Human Children Bedtime 8pm and pinned it the wall in his room. After that the pixies let him sleep.

Also, let the Fairies know you need to sleep. I put an aspirin on the corner of my bed stand every night when I lived in a house in the country. This was my sign to the Fairies no partying after ten o'clock at night. They can be quite the partiers. It is awesome, but every person needs rest. Fairies don't. They are constantly celebrating everything. This is why your child will feel elated to speak about them. You also will become elated during the conversation.

Love yourself and your children enough to be open and ready to receive messages and gifts from these wondrous beings that see the wondrousness of you!

Fairies tend to hang out around your feet. They are your connection to the earth around you. As you start to see them note how they organize around your feet.

If they are in a circle pattern, things are good and you make your intentions heard and clear.

If they are in a square pattern, you demand heavily out of your Fairies and you need to let them do their job. Basically, you turned your Fairies into a military.

If the Fairies more resemble a cloud, this is because the Fairies are restless and need organization.

The more restless or bored a fairy is, the more likely they are to go rogue. A rogue fairy will appear as if a fairy is out of place.

When a rogue fairy is left unchecked or unaddressed, the more likely they are to turn into a gremlin. Now a gremlin is still technically a fairy, but they are trying to use any means necessary to get your attention.

If you want to keep your Fairies happy, make your intentions plain and clear. Once you've made your intentions, release them to the universe. Write your intentions down and let them go.

Make a place in your garden or house especially for the Fairies. I have a special bookshelf where most of my fairies live. There are other places they like, my plants, the seashells and crystals I have collected and near my wands.

I have seen Fairy Gardens in yards, specific places you create just for them. In one of my yards I wrapped clothe ribbons around the branches of shrubs with seashells, beads and bells hanging from the ribbons. This was my offering to the fairies. My garden grew the best veggies that year.

In my flower garden, I planted holly hock seeds from France. I threw out semi- precious stone chips and tumbled stones into the garden as my offerings to the Fairies. Every year people would drive up my driveway to see my beautiful nine - foot tall hollyhock flowers.

One year a rose bush appeared in my garden. I am horrible with growing roses. This rose bush took off and bloomed and bloomed! It was so pretty. It was a gift from the fairies!

You can leave offerings for them, they love flowers, sparkly objects and chocolate. Do not be surprised if your offerings are missing the next day. Watch as your garden or houseplants flourish.

The best time to see the Fairies is during sunrise or sunset. They love this time of day as this is the time when the realms overlap. During this time take a breath with your child and open yourself to see the Fairies living in and around your home. If you are drawn to a certain part of the yard or your home, take a breath, be still, be open and ready to receive their messages.

Fairies teach us to take care of, admire and appreciate our entire wondrous planet.

Take pictures, you might see orbs in the pictures. I know many people who do this and they have outstanding pictures of the Fairies that live with and around them.

FAIRY GODMOTHER

The Fairy Godmother inspires us always to do better and sprinkles us with inspiration.

Our Fairy Godmothers guide us towards our dreams and line up events to help us achieve our goals. So, if you are working on something and it doesn't seem to be moving fast enough you can call upon your Fairy Godmother to assist you with your endeavor.

Our Fairy Godmothers teach us about grace, how to be gracious and the wisdom of grace.

My Fairy Godmother assists me with my goals, intentions and reminds me all the time to be patient as the intentions for my highest good are fulfilled.

When I lived in Pagosa Springs, I wanted to buy a house. The loan I was approved for made my choices very limited. I was about to give up, but I kept feeling I needed to keep looking. I found my house on a county road very close to town, it was a back road I took as a shortcut. I can't believe I drove past the house all the time and didn't see it. On this day, I was inspired to slow down and look.

I had no credit, I had a part time job, was doing readings and selling jewelry.

Three months later, we were moving in before the biggest snowstorm of that year! I believe my Fairy Godmother inspired me to drive slower and look around the neighborhood! It was an awesome neighborhood! The house was such a blessing in our lives!

Every person on this planet has a Fairy Godmother. If you look at your life and how it has played out you will recognize the intervention of your Fairy Godmother. Now that you are aware of her why don't you say thank you for all the wondrous events she has helped you with?

Contacting your Fairy Godmother

Take a breath and quiet your mind.

Visualize a vortex or tornado circling your feet.

With each breath you take, the vortex rises over your body sinning faster and faster.

As the vortex spins you allow it to pull out of your field all those thoughts and energies that no longer serve you.

Visualize the vortex move up over your legs, hips, core, neck and head until you hear a pop. Your energetic field is now clear!

YAY!

Take a deep breath. Breathe in your favorite color and start to fill yourself with the color. Start with your toes. Keep filling your physical body with the color until you are full.

When you can 'see' the color coming out the ends of your hair and the pores of your skin, you're present and in your body.

I invite and invoke my Fairy God Mother to come forth and touch my left shoulder.

Be patient and allow your fairy Godmothers energy to approach you. You may feel her brush against your left shoulder. This is where the Fairy Godmother will reside in your energy field

When she is with you, you will feel uplifted and calm. What does she look like? Ask her what her name is. What is her message to you today? Remember to say thank you before you release her.

Explain to your children what a Fairy Godmother is; use Fairy tales to give examples.

Ask your children about their Fairy Godmothers. What does she look like? Do they receive messages from their Fairy Godmothers? Have them write it down and put it somewhere they can see it daily.

Watch as yours and their Fairy Godmothers help you create your best lifetime!

NOTES

GUARDIAN ANGEL

Your Guardian Angel is there to guard, guide and protect you. Many people associate this kind of Angel with the Archangel Michael. These Angels are his Angels, his legions. When you feel uneasy, connect with your Guardian Angel and ask for guidance. These Angels are wondrous beings.

They will give you assurance and advice according to the situation. You should follow their direction. There have been a couple instances in my life that I have truly felt uneasy and I have called upon my Guardian Angel for assistance. I received and followed his guidance very much to my relief. I am thankful for my Guardian Angel.

My Guardian Angel's name is Damiel. I call him Lord Damiel. We have traveled together many lifetimes. We have a close bond, I often hear him walking beside me. When there is someone near me who doesn't have the best intentions, I hear Damiel's metal wings fall around me. When I hear that sound, I know to be alert.

When I became aware of Lord Damiel, my guardian Angel. I was awed by his magnificence. I knew immediately he was an Angel. His wings are huge, metallic, silver and gold. He truly has been a blessing in my life. He is very much my guard and protector. Of all my Spirit Guides and Angels, Lord Damiel is the only one who consistently takes form.

I was on the bus, on my way home one night when a bunch of thugs got on. They were messing with everyone on the bus. Intimidating people and just being awful. I tried to make myself small, I was sitting in a window seat. They were heading my way. I grabbed my big purse, I kept a big rock in my big purse for occasions like this. If you swing your purse around in a perfect arch with enough force you can and will knock a person out. Yes, I know this from experience. I was raised in L.A. I learned how to be resourceful.

I heard a loud crashing sound, similar to metal doors being rolled down into place and I felt like I was encircled in a shroud of heavy protection. I heard Archeia Faith say, 'stay put'. I wasn't sure if she was talking to me because I didn't 'hear' her the way I normally 'hear' her.

Suddenly the whole pack of thugs stopped walking toward where I was sitting and turned around and found places to sit. Well you can imagine how relieved the people around me felt, including me. I was very thankful to Faith. She acknowledged me and also mentioned I should say thank you to Lord Damiel, my guardian Angel.

That's how I became aware of Lord Damiel. It never occurred to me I had a Guardian Angel until that night.

You also can get to know your Guardian Angel. Your guardian angel may not look like an angel.

Our Guardian Angels are our Guards; they guide us and protect us. It is their focus to keep us safe on all levels.

There have been other students who see Vikings, Native American Indians, Firemen, Samurai, animals, dragons, etc.

Now are you ready to meet your Guardian Angel?

Are you ready to develop a relationship with your Guardian Angel?

To meet your Guardian Angel

Take a breath and quiet your mind.

Visualize a vortex or tornado circling your feet.

With each breath you take, the vortex rises over your body sinning faster and faster.

As the vortex spins you allow it to pull out of your field all those thoughts and energies that no longer serve you.

Visualize the vortex move up over your legs, hips, core, neck and head until you hear a pop. Your energetic field is now clear!

YAY!

Take a deep breath. Breathe in your favorite color and start to fill yourself with the color. Start with your toes. Keep filling your physical body with the color until you are full.

When you can see the color coming out of the ends of your hair, the pores of your skin, you're present and in your body.

I invite and invoke my guardian angel to come forth and touch my right shoulder.

When you feel your Guardian Angel you will feel as though you are being held in a firm embrace of support and love. You may even see a beautiful metallic shield or wings all around you.

Explain to your child what a Guardian Angel is.

Have they seen their Guardian Angel?

Have them take a breath and center themselves. Then ask them to call to their Guardian Angel. What did they see/feel/hear?

NOTES

WHAT IS AN ENERGY VAMPIRE

It is a person who sucks up every one's energy around them by complaining, moaning, groaning, whining, manipulating, etc.! This person is someone who wants to look better than everyone else. They will try to make themselves look better by talking down about others. They are the petty tyrants and the bullies.

Everyone knows an energy vampire. They are everywhere. Most of the time they don't have a clue as to what they are. Those that do – beware!

I have met A LOT of intuitive people who are energy vampires. They will draw you in through manipulation and take advantage of you.

I knew this gal who was an energy worker, psychic medium. Every darn time I saw her she was after me trying to put me in a place of fear that I had a demon attached to me.

She saw me channel the Archeia Hope once and asked how she could overcome evil. Archeia Hope told her to stop talking about it. The more she spoke about it the more she drew it to herself. After that she was going around telling everyone I was channeling the devil!

This woman would draw in her clients with scare tactics and try to make them feel bad for not attending all of her events.

If you know an intuitive person like that, walk away, just walk away!

After being around them you will feel tired, maybe annoyed and frustrated.

How do they become like this?

Most of the time it is learned from parents and families. This how they learned how to get attention.

What to do to assist an Energy Vampire shift their position-

*Say to them - Hey, find a different way of getting my attention! Keep reminding them, give them positive examples of how to get your attention.

*Limit the time you spend with that person(s).

*Wrap them in a pink bubble of Love. - This works and often times they will walk away mid - sentence!

* Do not allow them to annoy you. This is the way they get your energy. It is your energy; your energy is for you! Instead smile at them and say -

Oh, let me consider what you have said!

You are still present with them but not agreeing with them. With that you can shift the subject to something more interesting.

Bullies - Some people mistake Bullies for Stalkers. Bullies are in a class of their own. They are so insecure about who they are, they are always trying to make a point to get attention or hold someone back by meanness. They are takers, they will eventually drain you dry - on all levels!

What do you do about a bully? Walk away. Ignore

them, do not give them any energy. Stand up to them in the most neutral position you can if it comes to that.

Many people are in relationships where one of the partners will keep the other poor emotionally and financially so they feel like they can't leave the partnership. How to resolve that? Dissolve the partnership. Leave. The partnership is not an equal exchange of energy. That should be the intention for all of your relationships.

Don't be a victim! Be a Superhero!

What can you do to bring in people for your highest good, that will be an equal exchange of energy?

Intend for new friends to come into your life. (It works, I do it with great results all the time)

Don't put a lot of energy into talking about the Energy Vampires. The less you talk about them the less you will meet them. Negativity breeds negativity.

Be Positive!

When you meet an Energy Vampire, put yourself in an egg. The egg can be any color you want it to be. With the intention of keeping your personal space clear of the negative energy. It works, I fluff out my egg all the time. Those people that are not for my highest good will turn around and walk away.

BOUNDARIES AND SELF PRESERVATION

Boundaries are what I call decisive action. It is you letting your friends, family, significant others and acquaintances know who you are.

We have friends and family, if you give them an inch they will definitely take a mile. They will wear us down with their demands and attitudes. We might do everything we can to please and appease them. Nothing will ever be good enough and we exhaust ourselves trying.

We think maybe if I try harder I can be a better guide to this person.

Stop!

Instead of bending over backward and doing all kinds of crazy acrobats, try setting up some boundaries with this person(s).

This is a 'be present and honor yourself' lesson.

Here is your checklist –

How do I feel when I am around this person(s)?

How do I feel after I leave this person(s)?

If you feel disrespected, disregarded, manipulated, tired, exhausted or despondent it is time to end the relationship or set your boundaries.

My advice if you decide the relationship is worth saving and you still want to assist the relationship set a time limit with your contact with this person. Set an egg timer, use your phone if it has a timer. Let the person know –

I have ten minutes to talk to you today.

Stick to your time limit, remember this person is used to getting what they want from you.

Many energetic vampires know exactly what they are doing and either are perfecting the art or have perfected it.

If you think you can help this person expand themselves and move out of this way of being with you, set those boundaries and stick to them.

Sometimes we have to walk away. We have to keep moving forward and let them go. Don't feel guilty. Trust the Universe, that there will be another person(s) who will come into their lives to help them out of the energetic vampire stage. What a great teacher they were for you, they taught you what you don't want so you can be open to what you do want!

Awesome, right?

I have had to walk away from people I love because I decided I have done everything I could to make this situation better. Yes, more than once it broke my heart. I mended and I am more present and decisive in my friendships now.

I learned over the years that the friendships have to be an Equal Exchange of Energy and more for me to get involved. If it is not an Equal Exchange of Energy I walk.

As you release old ways of being, you make room for more of what is for your highest good. Your vibration or resonance rises and you expand and grow. You will start to attract more people into your life who match your resonance.

Yes, there will be those who you will leave behind. That's okay, if they want to be in your circle make them stretch and grow too. Do not lower your vibration to be around them.

Honoring yourself brings balance in your life. Be a great example to the people around you.

This is the only lifetime I will be Auriel Grace and I want the rest of this lifetime to be joyful, full of wonder and more!

This is a decision you can make too!

HOME IS SANCTUARY

Housekeeping is not my favorite activity. It is something that I have worked on my adult life. Yes, we are going to talk about housekeeping.

Look around your home, what do you like about it?

Do you still have those ugly pillows your mother in law gave you? Do they annoy you?

Your home should not be annoying, it is your sanctuary from the world.

When I start working with people they grow and change. We start to be more aware of what brings us peace.

My clients start cleaning and clearing their homes or they may change homes.

I have learned over the years I like my home to be neat and clean. I like it because it keeps everything clear. I like clarity. I don't keep things. If I don't use things I give them away. I am not a collector.

I have noticed those homes that are full of clutter are full of dense energy.

One of the first questions I ask a psychic kid –

Is your bedroom clean?

If it isn't, their first homework assignment is to clean and organize their rooms.

I knew this gal who was ALWAYS broke. She had quite the collection of EVERYTHING in her house. One day she was fussing to me about paying her house payment. I told her to sell one of the three freezers she had that she wasn't using to pay her house payment. She looked at me like I struck her in the face!

You know that gal sold her freezer and liked doing it so much she started her own business in her yard buying and selling household items and furniture. She doesn't complain about money no more and her home is neat and clean. She sold the clutter out of her home.

Start cleaning your homes of anything not serving and you don't like to create peace and harmony in your house. Get a Feng Shui person to walk through your house to help you. Feng Shui can change your life. It has changed mine several times.

Got the theme of this chapter?

I also have some handy tips especially for those of you who have haunted or energetically challenged homes.

Kosher Salt in a glass or wood bowl centrally located in your home. It absorbs frustration, anger and residual unwanted energy.

Roses raise the resonance of the house. The smell of roses will soothe and calm you and your family. The smell of roses keep the vibration high in your home. The scent of roses is the scent of unconditional love, the highest vibration of all.

Ringing bells in the corners of your home breaks up residual energy. String up some jingle bells on a leather strip and ring them once a month in your house. If you have a family living in the house you will want to do this more often.

Monster spray in the bedrooms for a good night's rest and to keep away the unwanted spirits. Monster Spray is good for adults too.

Now to guard and protect your home you will want to invoke the Arch Angel Michael and Archeia Faith. They will guard and protect your house.

I invite and invoke Archangel Michael and Archeia Faith to protect my house for the highest greatest good of myself and my family. Guide guard and protect myself, spouse and children always. Thank you!

When you ask them to protect your house you will see a fence of Angels surrounding your house. You may even see them standing on the rooftop.

If you move, invite Archangel Michael and Archeia Faith to follow you to protect your next house. Remember to greet them and always give thanks for their protection. Don't be surprised if you hear them say you are welcome or you may feel blissed out for the day! This is quite wondrous in itself.

You will know your house is being protected by the Angels because you feel at peace in your house no matter the circumstance.

Remember the Angels were created to assist mankind. They see every living being as special and wondrous. They love to help. Open yourself to them and you will see wondrous events happen in your life.

To keep out unwanted energy or spirits in your home, visualize waterfalls in your windows and doorways. You want to make sure your energy waterfalls are lightly flowing waterfalls. This will clear off any spirits or energies you, your family or friends may have in their energy field before you enter your home.

You will also find by putting all these concepts in place those people who do not serve your family will not be able to come inside your home or if they get in, they will not stay.

All of these concepts can be used for your work or business as well.

I had a client who was a mortician. He and his wife had a horrible time keeping their house clear of unwanted spirits. When I went in to clear their home I visualized the waterfalls in all the windows and entrances of the house. I let them know to strengthen the waterfalls a couple of times a month to keep out the unwanted spirits. After that clearing, they had a bright, high vibrational home, they felt safe in.

Creating a peaceful, harmonious environment in your home assists you with rest and peace in your life.

NOTES

INTENTION AND LIVING INTENTIONALLY

All intuitive and energy work is done through intention. When I start a session and I am connecting to my spirit guides and angels, I ask that all messages are for the highest and greatest good of my client. When I am setting up home and office I ask for the highest good too. This book is set up for yours and my highest and greatest good.

Sometimes what we see is for our highest good doesn't jive with us in the moment, but wait when the situation clears, you see it is for your highest good! Look back at your life and you will see situations that have come up and you thought, how the heck did I get into this? Then suddenly everything turns around and there you were safe and sound. The Creator, Universe, God really does have your back. Being present and aware of your decisions backs it up!

Making Intentions and Living Intentionally is an awesome endeavor. What does it mean to make Intentions and be open to the flow of the Universe?

Kids do it all the time. They ask for stuff and they move

along with their day staying open and ready to receive whatever it is they want. This is second nature for kids, especially if they are confident about what they want.

When my son Xander was eight years old, he decided he wanted to learn how to fish. We were camping by the Taos River at the time and he saw someone fishing. He stated his desire. The next day a man pulled up in an old, brown Ford, got out, opened his trunk and asked, "Who wanted to learn how to fish?"

Xander received a fishing pole, a tackle box, a hat, and a fish bag. How awesome is that? Xander opened himself to the flow and received what he asked for.

Children are very good at manifesting, they think about what they want and it always comes to them. Encourage them to manifest whatever they want. Always remind them to ask for their Highest and Greatest Good and believe the Universe will provide them with whatever they need and more.

You can be good at manifesting, too. Believing in what you ask for and being grateful when you get it is very important when making Intentions. Following through and surrendering yourself to the Universal Flow or Divine Source are the biggest steps you need to make.

You can live intentionally, and teach people how to make Intentions by being an example. If you make personal and Universal Intentions, you align with your family's and friends' Intentions. It is fun to see the Universe fulfill your desires.

When the Universe gives something to you, say thank you and treat the situation, property, or person wondrously. You asked for it, so be sure to love it and be genuinely thankful.

My friend Vicki made me aware of intentions. She taught me to say my intentions daily. While I knew her in

Pagosa Springs, I saw her manifest her lifestyle. She decided one day she wanted a boyfriend to come into her life that liked to travel, was creative and open to creating a great life. It took her about six months.

I actually met him first through an intention circle at a friend's house. I told Vicki all about it. Vicki went with me for the second circle. I introduced them and they immediately clicked. They did travel around teaching groups about Intention and running Intention Circles. It was awesome!

Vicki decided at one time to intend for an R.V. to come to her freely, easily and effortlessly. They traveled around for about two months with her saying her intention, at the last intention circle the reverend there gave her an R.V.

While you are creating your own intentions please make sure to put into them, freely, easily and effortlessly. Those are powerful words too and those words help you to be open to receiving from expected and unexpected sources.

Example of General Personal Intentions

I Intend and I am so very grateful my children are Healthy, Happy, Whole, Guided, Guarded and Protected and Connected to our own Divine Source.

I intend my career(s) is fun, fulfilling, prosperous, and abundant for myself, my family.

I intend and I am grateful that I am peaceful, harmonious, energetic, courageous, kind, joyous, successful, creative, loving and young.

I intend and I am grateful my heart is always open and I am aligned with love. I am grateful for my family, extended family, friends new and old.

I intend and am grateful for all the wondrous synchronistic events that have happened and will happen in my life.

I intend I recognize and act upon synchronistic events to expand my prosperity and abundance on all levels.

I intend the quality of my life is beyond my wildest dreams.

I intend all of my intentions come to me freely, easily and effortlessly, from expected and unexpected sources!

I say these Intentions and Gratitude's for the highest and greatest good to the Universe, for myself and everyone involved!

Do you align with me?

So be it, so it is!

Every time one of your Intentions comes about, remember to say thank you!

Being thankful is huge it helps to raise your vibration. When you raise your vibration, you open yourself for more of what you want to happen in your life. I love saying thank you to the Universe!

Remember, you can ask for anything. Do not limit your experiences. If it is for your highest good it will happen.

Participate in Random Acts of Kindness, and participation in these Acts will help extend and expand yourself in great ways.

What is a Random Act of Kindness? Opening doors for people, saying something nice to someone, giving chocolate, hugs, and kisses (everyone loves the vibration of good lovin'), bringing ease and compassion to those in need. These are everyday miracles. Please do not overlook them; be thankful for them.

Living intentionally is good for every being living on this Planet Earth and Planet Earth Herself. She is, after all, a living entity. Remember, you leave an energetic path everywhere you go. In other words, we leave a little bit of ourselves everywhere we go. So, remember to be in a good place, no matter where you are, and take care of yourself and your environment in the best way you can.

Here are some examples:

So, remember to be in a good place, no matter where you are, and take care of yourself and your environment in the best way you can. Here are some examples:

I recycle (when I can) and use recycled materials.

When I lived in the country I grew gardens, I love organic gardening and organic food.

I harvested flower seeds from my gardens and then walked up and down my street throwing the seeds as I walked. Everyone loves flowers!

I pick up litter.

I download media and music instead of buying magazines and books (paper companies create horrible pollution in our rivers).

I buy from and donate to thrift stores. Recycle, Reuse, Reinvent

I educated myself and my family about sustainable living. I've encouraged people to "go green" in building their houses with as many natural materials as they can.

I encouraged people to figure out how their house can make good use of sunshine and solar panels, windmills, water-catch systems, well water, and good insulation will help heat and cool the house in all seasons.

Doing all errands in one trip, to carpool, walk, bicycle and use hybrid cars. I believe the more we educate ourselves and our families about our environment and how to take care of it, the better we will feel about our surroundings and ourselves.

These are ideas for living with the Highest and Greatest good for all. Pretty simple, really, isn't it? What are your ideas for living intentionally?

ASSIGNMENT

What are your Intentions? What are you grateful for? Write them down, proclaim them aloud! You can write intentions on sticky notes and put them in' places you will see them in your home. Have a vision board on your bedroom wall. Add to it all the time. You are the creator of your life – do you want a happily ever after? Who doesn't?

In doing this exercise you can really figure out what you want in your life. Stay focused and flexible because you never know what wondrous event is right around the corner waiting for you to discover it!

NOTES

CRYSTALS & PENDULUMS

When choosing a pendulum, continue to remember that it is an extension of you. It is like choosing a crystal or any tool that you use. Choose the pendulum that makes you feel joyous at first sight or make your own.

A pendulum is made with one large stone on one end and a smaller stone on the other with either chain or beads between the ends. The pendulum is a tool you can use to ask your higher self, yes and no questions.

A pendulum can be made out of anything. You can even use your keys.

When you start to use a pendulum, it might not swing. Relax so the pendulum will swing. Consider the pendulum is an extension of yourself; it is you communicating with Divine Source and receiving guidance.

Take a breath, close your eyes and be open and ready to receive your answers.

It is amazing when kids pick up a pendulum. They can get their pendulums swinging within seconds. They love asking to see the directions of their yes, no, and maybe, and watch the pendulum swing. It is awesome!

Why use a Pendulum?

The pendulum that you choose and use is an extension of yourself and a tool to help you connect to your Higher Self to receive information for your highest and greatest good.

You can use pendulums to help you with these types of questions.

Choose – the correct foods, the best mate, the correct time for action

Find – missing objects, the best job, the best housing or schools

Discover – compatible relationships, personal and business/Existing or potential

Make – accurate business, personal or spiritual decisions or the best consumer choices.

USING A PENDULUM

The way to use a pendulum is to suspend the small end of the pendulum between your thumb and first two fingers. Ask for a demonstration of a "yes" answer, a "no" answer, then a "neutral" answer. Remember which way your pendulum swings for your yes, no and neutral. This is how you will receive the answers to your questions. Keep your mind clear and detached from the outcome.

Remember, as with any skill, this requires practice and patience.

Phrase your questions as statements. For example,

"It is for my Highest Good to see this movie, read this book, meet this person, eat this food,"

Or you can say,

"My unborn child is female"

Or

"My keys are in the living room."

Observe the swing of your pendulum for your answer.

Before you begin your work with your pendulum, clear yourself by saying a prayer, or set an Intention. For example, you can say,

"I ask this work is for the Highest Good of myself, All Beings Everywhere, and the Universe,"

Or

"I ask this work be in the Light of God/Goddess and in the Highest Interests of All concerned."

In all cases, remember to breathe, relax, and have fun.

NOTES

CRYSTALS, GEMS & MINERALS

I am always asked what crystals should I always have with me or in my house. I always want to say as many as you like and love! However my practical answer is this -

Clear Quartz Crystal – Positive energy stone. Keeps the energy field clear and positive.

Amethyst – Spiritual Stone – Assists with connecting to our higher selves, spirit guides, angels and source. Helps us overcome addictions. Assists with lucid dreaming.

Citrine – Happiness, prosperity and abundance.

Smokey Quartz – Clears negativity from people and property. Clears itself.

Selenite – Todd calls this stone the shopvac stone. What he means is that it sucks out all the negativity out of your energy field and leaves you with a feeling of peace.

Obsidian – Protection stone, clears itself.

Rose Quartz – Friendship, love, heart stone

Starting with these stones in different areas of your home can shift the energy immediately. I have several sets of these stones always in the home. They are in the bedroom, living room and the office space of our home. They have their own bowls or shelves they reside in. This combination of stones is great for everyone.

It really doesn't matter the form of the crystals. If you like big crystals, buy big crystals. If you like tumbled stones, buy tumbled stones. The energy in the stones does not diminish or increase because of the size. The stones are for your home, pick the stones that truly resonate with you.

I also have several wands that I have programed for bringing in new inspirations, prosperity and abundance, keeping the house clear and sparkly and for connecting to the Divine.

Programming crystals or wands is easy. Hold the wand or crystal and focus on it. State your intention for it and focus on the crystal or wand. You will feel a shift when the crystal has accepted the programming.

Take care of your stones, making sure they are dusted and in clean areas.

Every six months or so I give all of my crystals a shower and set them outside for charging right before full moon. I keep them outside until a couple days after full moon. They like that it sparks them right up. You will feel the difference in your home when you bring them inside.

Wear your favorite stones too. Remember jewelry also needs to be cleaned and maintained too. Take care of it, so it can take care of you.

There are a lot of great books out there about crystals, their virtues, geology and minerology. Learn about your stones.

Always make sure with the precious stones you are getting what you are paying for. Make sure there is certification and you can insure those precious pieces. Go to a certified gemologist to purchase those high - end stones.

I encourage everyone to discover the crystal realm. It is

fun to learn about where they come from and their histories. Their histories are yours too. The Earth is wondrous and mysterious. The crystals can teach us about where they come from and what their virtues are if we are open to understand their energy.

PLAYING AND SIMPLIFYING

Paul David, a teacher and friend to me, counseled me on many occasions about playing and to teach other adults how to play. I have done some work with adults with soul retrieval in helping to bring out their inner child. As a result, I have coached people on how and why we need to play.

Playing is for everyone! Allowing our imagination to flow and relaxing in the flow is a great gift. This is a great way to open yourself to the flow of the Universe and help your intentions come true.

It is hard to find time to play, especially adults who are responsible for children and home. We have to pay bills, grocery shopping and do housework etc. All of those chores are things that can be done as the day goes on, make a list of all your tasks get them done or assign specific times to do them. Simplify your life by making chore lists for yourself and family. Explain to your family as soon as chores are done there is more time together for fun!

You know it is easier to be happy than distraught, just like it takes fewer muscles to smile than to frown. A lot of adults really need to be present and in their bodies. What this means is paying attention to what is going on around you all the time. If you don't like what is going on in your life, then change it. You are the only one who can do it for yourself.

You are in charge of your Happily Ever After!

I used to play with my kids. My favorite thing to do with my kids was to play video games. I always had them beat the bosses in the games and show me how to work the controls and all the fun things that went with the video games. They usually did this while they ate dinner and it was fun. We loved playing together.

Many parents find it hard to do these things because they feel like they have to be serious adults. Being serious is not fun. There is a time and place for everything, so give yourself permission to have fun. I do it all the time.

In my life, I have learned how to make money having fun, besides doing readings and soul retrieval, I used to design jewelry and Fairies and sell them. My favorite food is Chocolate, most of my regular jobs have been in candy stores having to do with chocolate.

I also write fiction novels. It helps me to play and be imaginative while creating income for my family. This helps me be the responsible, reliable adult I am while having fun and playing.

We know people are not the same and we all have our different ways of playing. Playing helps the inner child of ours be happy and helps the whole being-ness be lighter and brighter. Figure out what it is you like to do and do it for at least fifteen – thirty minutes a day.

I have worked with a lot of people who look at me like I am crazy when I tell them – part of your problem is you don't play. You don't have fun. Most of the time people don't know what their fun is. Part of fun is discovering what we enjoy. By discovering what your fun is you start to simplify your life by getting rid of non- fun activities. We are always maturing and growing. Are tastes change.

I had a client who wanted to know why she wasn't happy. She was very successful and busy. She had the trophy house and the great family. She enjoyed her career. She and her husband were cash poor. She wasn't having any fun. When I pointed out she was lacking fun and romance in her life. She was so stunned, she started crying.

In six month's she and her husband sold their trophy house, bought a smaller practical house. Got rid of non-essential items, created schedules so they could have fun as a couple. The next time I saw her she was genuinely smiling and ready for her next adventure.

Consider your life, are you living your life for someone else or are you living your life for yourself?

Here are some ideas

Drawing, coloring, painting, sculpture, gardening, playing video games or board games (especially with kids), eating an ice cream cone, dancing, if you can think of it, do it, at least try it. Make it fun and light! You are playing!

Keeping a journal – this helps release stuff from the day, clears the mind and the heart.

Create a dream board or book – go crazy with it – it is yours. Use stickers, magazine cuttings, glitter, colored pens etc.

As you do these little fun suggestions you will feel clear and lighter, the lighter you are the brighter you are, shine your light!

Remember this is our own Heaven on Earth – Celebrate your life and have fun with it!

Isn't that why you came here, to live your dreams and shine your light?

NOTES

EQUAL EXCHANGE OF ENERGY

This is the last part of this book because you need to think about your life and how it is progressing.

What is an Equal Exchange of Energy?

Equal exchange of energy is a part of our daily lives. It is our love, friends, business and family relationships.

An Equal Exchange of Energy is a balanced relationship, sales transaction, trade etc. You walk away feeling good about what you just did, whether it was buying a dress, business or career move or having a relationship that blooms.

In a career as an Intuitive Advisor and Healer we have found people in the world will argue about paying for a reading, healing or workshop. Their reason is that God gave this gift and it should be given freely...hmmm, is that an equal exchange of energy?

No.

Paying the Carpenter for his labor or paying for a book

is an equal exchange of energy for services. People do this every day and they are o.k. with it. Why is it so hard for some people to pay for the services of their Intuitive Reader/ Counselor?

During creation, the Divine Ones gave us all the gift of intuition and insight. Every being is different and chooses how deep they want to go with the gift.

Those of us who have chosen to take our gifts to higher levels have also studied and learned how to apply what we have learned just as a doctor, lawyer, carpenter or clerk. This is our career, just like you have a career and get paid for it. So, when you are thinking of getting a reading, remember you do have to pay for it by currency or trade. Make it an equal exchange of energy.

An equal exchange of energy is not just for careers it is for every aspect of your life. There are many Intuitive people making a living as Readers and their families do not support them, the family is critical and fearful of what people think.

It doesn't matter what other people think about you. What matters is how you feel about you. Once you make that shift, you will meet people who will appreciate you.

If you feel as though you are giving more and more and there is not a return in your relationships, it is time to take a look at them and ask yourself do you feel tired or ill when you are around these friends and family of yours. If you do it is time to take some space and decide if these relationships are for your highest good.

Are they? If not it is time to put your energy in a place where there is an equal exchange.

When there is an equal exchange of energy you flourish on all levels. You will find that your heart is lighter and you feel bright and beautiful just being the wondrous person that you are. Be courageous and start making the moves to make your life joyous no matter how long it takes or how far you go. You are here on this planet, this heaven on earth to learn, feel, think and experience this life in joy! What are you waiting for?

Be courageous, be wondrous, be YOU!

ARE YOU PRESENT?

You have taken the first steps. When you are present everything just starts flowing and you are the one making responsible decisions clearly.

Flexing those intuitive muscles every day, keeps you fit and present in your life. You have that intuition built into you so you can make those great decisions for your higher and better good.

Be Present and Create that Happily Ever After – whatever that may be! You have the ability and now some tools for your toolbox. Use them every day. That's why you have intuition.

Our kids need to see us in our Divinity so they will do the same. We are their greatest examples. They need to see us being unconditional so they can give themselves permission to do the same. Your children chose you as their parents, honor them, show them your Divinity and allow them theirs.

GLOSSARY OF TERMS

This is some of the vocabulary that is used and its respective meaning. This is written so that you the reader will have a reference and an understanding and some clarity of what is being discussed.

Akashic Records – In a location outside of time and space there is a library where everything is written down and accessible. If someone looks up your Akashic record, they are looking up all information about your soul, current, past and present.

Angel – Beings of Pure Light and Love who serve as messengers from our Divine Source

Ascension – A constant learning process through our lives as we come closer and closer to the Light. Every living being has the opportunity to Ascend!

Ascended Master – Spiritually enlightened beings who in past incarnations were ordinary humans, but who have undergone a process of spiritual transformation. The Ascended Masters have a great understanding of the human condition.

Aura – The energetic field that is the halo of light around a person, place or thing. The energetic field
    can be multicolored or one solid color, depending on the object or living being. The aura or energy field can fluctuate in color if the human being is ill or experiencing different emotions.

An example is if a person is a smoker, the energy is usually closer to the body and there are black specks in it. If a person has cancer or some kind of chronic illness the spots are reflected in the aura.

Chakras – The seven energy centers of the body. Each Chakra has its own purpose and color and should be about two inches in diameter. The Chakra looks like a beautiful spinning vortex.

Channel – A trance channel is a person who fully incorporates an Ascended Master or Angelic.

Clairalience – Using your nose and your sense of smell, you can retrieve information. Some spirits have a certain scent that can be associated with them. Clairalience is the ability to detect these scents.

Clairaudience – To hear intuitively past our three-dimensional world clearly, hearing those who have passed over, Angels, guides, etc. Many of our mentally ill people are clairaudient and clairvoyant. It is not a linear way of being so their senses are dulled by medication prescribed to them by psychologists and medical doctors.

Claircognizance – 'Clear Knowing' as it is also knowing, is the ability to recognize and receive information from the ethers without dismissing it. Most Prophets are Claircognizant.

Clairgustance – 'You can literally taste it.' Clairgustance is the ability to taste information.

Clairsentience – 'Psychometry' is the ability to feel or touch objects or persons and receive knowledge about those objects or a person story.

Clairvoyance – The ability to see past our three-dimensional holographic world clearly. For example: Ghosts, Angels, Fairies, Spirit Guides, etc. As you work through the clarity classes you will develop sensitivity to seeing such things.

Disincarnate(s) – Ghosts. A human being who has died and their spirit are still on this earth plane. Many times, these spirits are still on Earth because they are lost or want resolution for the life they left.

Empathic – The ability to recognize and understand feelings of another person or persons.

Ether/Etheric or The Fifth Element – The place where Akashic information is stored is in the Etheric. It is all around us.

Fairy or Elemental – These are the teachers, guides and

helpers of the earth. There are Fairies everywhere and are denoted by the four earth elements.

Sylphs – Fairies of air.
    Undines – Fairies of water.
    Salamanders – Fairies of fire.
    Gnomes – Fairies of earth.

Fairies range in all kinds of shapes and sizes. What is wondrous about Fairies is there is no hierarchy. All Fairies know their own importance and the importance of all other living beings.

Fwomp – Energy work either by fixing something, removing something, or adjusting something energetically.

Higher Self – The eternal core or essence of every living being.

Intuition – To take information from the ethers and interpret it in regards to self or others.

Invite – To give permission. It is a verbal allowance.

Invoke – To call for with earnest desire, pray for, and a way to bring in Archangels. When calling the angels, we both invite and invoke them.

Magic – To take something that is nonphysical and brings it into the physical.

Magician – A person who practices magic. All intuitive arts are performed by magicians who bring information from the ethers into the physical world.

Medium – An Etheric Information Gatherer. The personal connection of bringing the spiritual into the physical is called mediumship.

Pixies – A type of fairy with difference in appearance, size and wing structure.

Reiki – A Japanese word meaning (Rei – Universal life force and Ki (or chi): Life Energy) Reiki is an energy modality that resorts energetic balance and sets an environment for wellness on all levels. That includes physical, mental, emotional and spiritual.

Resonate – To understand what another is saying or being in either unison or in harmony.

Sorcerer – A magician who is in it for themselves.

Spirit Guides – Beings from many places, including past life friends, family members, angels, Fairies, and other dimensional beings that help guide us throughout our lifetimes.

Telepathy – Communication between minds.

Unconditional – There are no ifs ands or buts attached to feeling. There are no limits. There are not requirements.

ABOUT THE AUTHOR

Auriel Grace is a natural intuitive. Since she was five years old, she has been able to see and communicate with spirit guides, angels, and other unseen beings.

In the late 1990's, she became a Reiki Master Teacher and received her ordainment under the Order of Melchizedek. The Order of Melchizedek is a spiritual organization where we seek health and well-being for all beings everywhere.

In 2004-2005, Auriel learned the art of Soul Retrieval, a way to Grace!

The year 2010 brought Auriel into helping people with their growth of consciousness by giving Deeksha Blessings.

Auriel Grace is also honored to be a Trance Channel for the Archeia, who are the Divine Compliments of the Arch Angels. Some of the Divine beings Auriel channels are Mother Mary, Lord Melchizedek and the Goddess Venus.

She has practiced all over the United States assisting people with connecting to their hearts desire and their happily every after's. She loves bringing the energy of Hope to the people she meets and works with. Auriel is constantly learning and growing in her practice as a Psychic and Soul Retrieval Practitioner.

www.aurielgrace.net

OTHER BOOKS BY AURIEL GRACE –

The Goddess Trilogy

The Book of Yzabelle

The Book of Ambyr

The Book of Bethany - 2022

These stories are lifetimes Auriel Grace has remembered and written!

Are you a part of those lifetimes?

Lucy Prophet is a series of a young lady with a vision and how she 'sees' that through! What would you do if you won the lottery?

Lucy Prophet Psychic Girl

Lucy Prophet Psychic Girl II

Lucy Prophet Psychic Girl III

Lucy Prophet Psychic Girls IV 12/2020

A Psychic's Story Series

Haunted – A Psychic's Story 10/31/2016

Angels – A Psychic Story 12/2016

I am Psychic, Not Telepathic – 11/2017

Clearing With Purpose Goo & Cooties 12/2018

Did you like I am Psychic, Not Telepathic? Please remember to leave a review on Amazon! Thank you!

Made in the USA
Middletown, DE
01 September 2024

60294505R00076